National Park Service
U.S. Department of the Interior

Shenandoah National Park
Luray, Virginia

Shenandoah National Park
Traveler Information Coordination Study

Upper photos Source: Shenandoah National Park. Lower Photos Source: US DOT Volpe Center (2003)

PMIS No. 145352
September 2011

John A. Volpe National Transportation Systems Center

U.S. Department of Transportation
Research and Innovative Technology Administration

Table of Contents

Introduction 1
Winter Road Closures 1
Entrance Station Congestion 1

Existing Conditions 3
Park Visitation 3
Park Access Routes and Entrance Stations 4
Congestion at Entrance Stations and on Access Routes 10
Skyline Drive Closures 12
Existing Traveler Information Systems 12

Evaluation of Strategies 17
Improved Traveler Information Regarding Skyline Drive Closures 17
Addressing Congestion at Park Entrances 21

Recommended Actions 26

Report Notes

This report was prepared by the U.S. Department of Transportation John A. Volpe National Transportation Systems Center, in Cambridge, Massachusetts. The project was led by Kenneth Miller of the Systems Operations and Assessment Division with support from Kathleen Sylvester of MacroSys.

This effort was undertaken in fulfillment of PMIS 145352, Shenandoah National Park: Traveler information Coordination Study. The project statement of work was included in amendment 1 of the interagency agreement between the National Park Service and the Volpe Center (F4505087777), signed in July 2009. This project was funded by the Park Roads and Parkways Program Category III.

Acknowledgements

The authors wish to thank the numerous organizations and individuals who graciously provided their time, knowledge and guidance in the development of this report including:

Shenandoah National Park

Steve Herzog
Karen Beck-Herzog
Karen Michaud
Robbie Brockwehl
Lyn Rothgeb
Sandra Rushing
Tracy Thetford

Virginia Department of Transportation

Scott Cowherd
Homer Coffman
Vernon Hoke

Executive Summary

Shenandoah National Park is located in northwestern Virginia, about 60 miles southwest of Washington, DC. The park comprises 308 square miles of land buffering the 105-mile long Skyline Drive. It stretches about 80 miles north to south. The Front Royal Entrance Station is located about 8 miles southeast of the I-81 / I-66 interchange. Approximately one-third of all vehicles that arrive at the park enter at the Front Royal Entrance Station, which is the most convenient entrance point for travelers arriving from Washington. This report focuses on identifying transportation information solutions to alert visitors approaching Shenandoah from the vicinity of Front Royal about potential park closures due to weather and congestions issues. With the current traveler information systems, most visitors don't find out about closures until they arrive at the park and it is difficult to alert visitors to alternative routes when congestion occurs, leading to frustrated and disappointed visitors.

Issues

On weekend days when fall foliage peaks (mid- to late October), Shenandoah can experience significant congestion at the Front Royal Entrance Station. The queue of cars waiting to enter the park causes congestion throughout the town of Front Royal and can create safety hazards. During peak weekends, the park adds additional staff to help expedite the entrance process; however, congestion persists and occasionally stretches back over eight miles to the I-66 interchange.

When they arrive, visitors may pay the entrance fee using cash or a credit card, or may proceed without paying if they have a valid pass. Staff reported that credit card purchases are slower than cash purchases (though DSL connections installed at Front Royal last year have sped up credit card transactions at that location). About 55 percent of visitors pay with cash, 10 percent pay by credit card, and about 35 percent re-enter with a previously purchased pass. State police, park rangers, and/or park fee program supervisors will sometimes request entrance station staff to waive entrance fees in order to reduce the congestion. While this tactic does increase throughput at the entrance station and generally helps to relieve the congestion, it is not seen as an ideal long-term solution since it significantly reduces the amount of revenue collected by the park.

Weather-related closures of Skyline Drive generally occur each winter, with the number of closings varying significantly from year to year. Weather conditions within the park are often much more severe than in surrounding areas because much of the park is at significantly higher elevations than surrounding areas. Park staff report that visitors often arrive at park entrance gates unaware of road closures within the park. The park would like to improve travel information during these events in order to reduce unnecessary travel and associated traveler frustration.

Current Traveler Information

Shenandoah provides travel information – entrance locations, travel directions, weather conditions, and operating hours – to prospective visitors in several ways: on the park's web site, through the park phone system, press releases, and using park-operated highway advisory radio (HAR). In 2009, the park also began to use Twitter to post whether Skyline Drive was closed. None of the existing directional signage to the park provides dynamic information. Currently HAR scripts advise travelers to expect delays at entrance stations during peak times; however, limited broadcast distances often preclude alternative entrance decisions by drivers. All of the existing information systems require travelers to anticipate adverse conditions within the park and seek out the information, rather than allowing the park to proactively reach out to all approaching visitors.

Strategies Evaluated

This report identified and evaluated the following ways of improving visitor information.

- Improved Traveler Information Regarding Skyline Drive Closures
    - Modify Use of Existing Traveler Information Systems
        - Use phone system, website and twitter to consistently announce closure information.
    - Participate in 511 Virginia Traveler Information System
        - Submit closure updates to the widely used 511 Virginia traffic information system, managed by Virginia Department of Transportation (VDOT).
    - Install Variable Message Signs
        - Coordinate with VDOT to identify existing variable message signs (VMS) or to identify new sites for VMS that could be used to alert visitors of road closures as they approach Shenandoah.

- Addressing Congestion at Park Entrances
    - Provide Congestion Information
        - Provide seasonal messages about congestion on the park website and phone system.
        - Use Portable VMS to suggest entering through Thornton Gap.
    - Increase Entrance Station Capacity and/or Queue Storage
        - Formalize a procedure for waiving entrance fees when congestion becomes problematic.
        - Install tandem entrance booths.
        - Re-direct exiting traffic and allow entering traffic to use both sides of the roadway
        - Widen Entrance
    - Discount Early and/or Late Arrivals on Peak Visitation Days

Recommendations

After analyzing the above options, the report recommends following through with the following recommendations.

1) Participate in 511 Virginia system (addresses closures and congestion)
   Establish communication procedure for providing information to VDOT Regional Operations Center for posting to the Virginia 511 system and prepare template messages for consistent information sharing.

2) Pursue use of permanent or portable VMS to display closure and/or congestion event information on key Shenandoah access routes. (addresses closures and congestion)
   Determine whether VDOT and Town of Front Royal would permit VMS to be used on:
   - VA 55 and/or 340 in Front Royal
   - VA 211 near Thornton Gap
   - VA 33 near Swift Run Gap, and/or
   - VA 250 near Rockfish Gap.

   Determine whether portable VMS could be rented from VDOT or others.

3) Provide congestion information through the Shenandoah website and phone system. 8
   - Post prominent notices on the park website and phone system throughout the fall season alerting travelers to the potential for delays at the Front Royal entrance station at peak times to help travelers anticipate congestion and plan accordingly.
   - Encourage visitors who will make a loop through the park to enter through Thornton Gap and exit through Front Royal.

4) Update Shenandoah procedures for disseminating information during Skyline Drive closures. (addresses closures)
    - Add 511 communication procedures, prioritize website updates, formalize use of Twitter, include Skyline Drive status as part of the phone system welcome message during the winter.
    - Record and store template messages for the Road Weather mailbox of the phone system describing Skyline Drive statuses that can be selected when closures occur.
    - Consider shifting responsibility for phone system updates down the communication tree to help manage communication center responsibilities. Phone system can be updated from remote locations.

Introduction

Shenandoah National Park is located in northwestern Virginia, about 60 miles southwest of Washington, DC. The park comprises 308 square miles of land buffering the 105-mile long Skyline Drive. It stretches about 80 miles north to south.

In 2005, the Volpe Center completed a transportation planning study for Shenandoah National Park that included an assessment of the methods used by the park to disseminate travel information. The study documented park travel information systems, identified gaps in traveler information, and recommended the following prioritized list of traveler information services considered most likely to improve the visitor experience:

- A systematic means of sharing information with gateway communities
- A toll-free phone system
- Participation in 511 Virginia
- Additional Park website information.

Shenandoah National Park has implemented components of these recommendations, including adding information to the park website about Skyline Drive closures that is updated at least once a day during weather-related closures. However, the park has ongoing concerns related to disseminating information about two types of seasonal events: weather-related closures of Skyline Drive, and Entrance Station congestion.

Winter Road Closures

Weather-related closures of Skyline Drive generally occur each winter, with the number of closings varying significantly from year to year[*]. Weather conditions within the park are often much more severe than in surrounding areas because much of the park is at significantly higher elevations than surrounding areas. Park staff report that visitors often arrive at park entrance gates unaware of road closures within the park. The Park would like to improve travel information during these events in order to reduce unnecessary travel and associated traveler frustration.

Entrance Station Congestion

On weekend days when fall foliage peaks (mid- to late October), Shenandoah National Park can experience significant congestion at the Front Royal Entrance station. The queue of cars waiting to enter the park causes congestion throughout the town of Front Royal and can create safety hazards. The Thornton Gap entrance station also experiences occasional congestion during the peak season. Park staff noted that visitors often arrive at park entrance gates frustrated by the delay and unaware of alternative routes they could have used to avoid congestion.

This study builds on the recommendations of the previous study by first assessing and documenting existing conditions and current systems and procedures for providing traveler information during weather-related road closures and entrance station congestion events. The subsequent section describes

---

[*] In 2008, Skyline Drive was closed for its entirety for 3 days; in 2009, it was entirely closed for 9 days; and in 2010, it was entirely closed for 21 days. The average number of days that a portion of Skyline Drive was closed ranges from 7 days to 13 days.

and evaluates options for managing winter road closures and entrance station congestion. The final section summarizes recommended actions for improving traveler information and addressing congestion related to these seasonal events at Shenandoah National Park.

Existing Conditions

Key conditions relevant to the seasonal events and traveler information at Shenandoah National Park are described in this section.

Park Visitation

According to the National Park Service Public Use Statistics Office[*], over one million visitors travel to Shenandoah National Park each year. As shown in Figure 1, while visitation has dropped significantly since the peak of nearly 2.8 million in 1978, it has been fairly steady for the last four years. Monthly visitation, shown in Figure 2, peaks in October when scenic views of fall foliage draw many visitors to the park. For example, Park visitation was about 225,000 in October of 2008, whereas winter visitation is typically quite low, with approximately 25,000 visitors per month.

A survey of Shenandoah visitors conducted in July 2001 found that most visitors (72 percent) were visiting Shenandoah for the first time during the past 12 months, including 40 percent who had not visited in the last five years. Only 8 percent were frequent visitors to the park, visiting at least five times in the last year. Though only 27 percent of visitors surveyed were Virginia residents, most visitors (73 percent) arrived from origins within Virginia on the day of the visit. Most out-of-state visitors to Shenandoah came from Maryland.

Figure 1
Shenandoah National Park Annual Visitation
Source: NPS Public Use Statistics Office

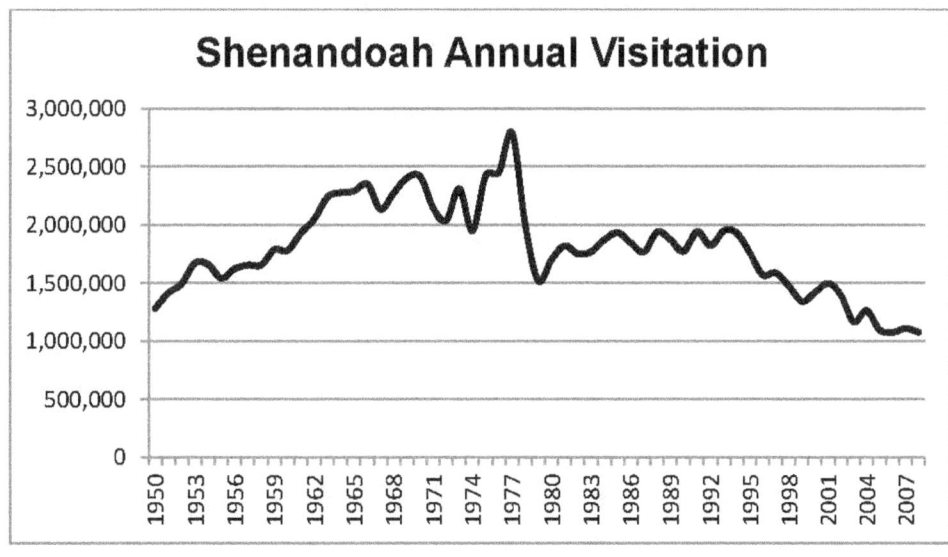

[*] http://www.nature.nps.gov/stats/park.cfm

Figure 2
Shenandoah National Park Monthly Visitation
Source: NPS Public Use Statistics Office

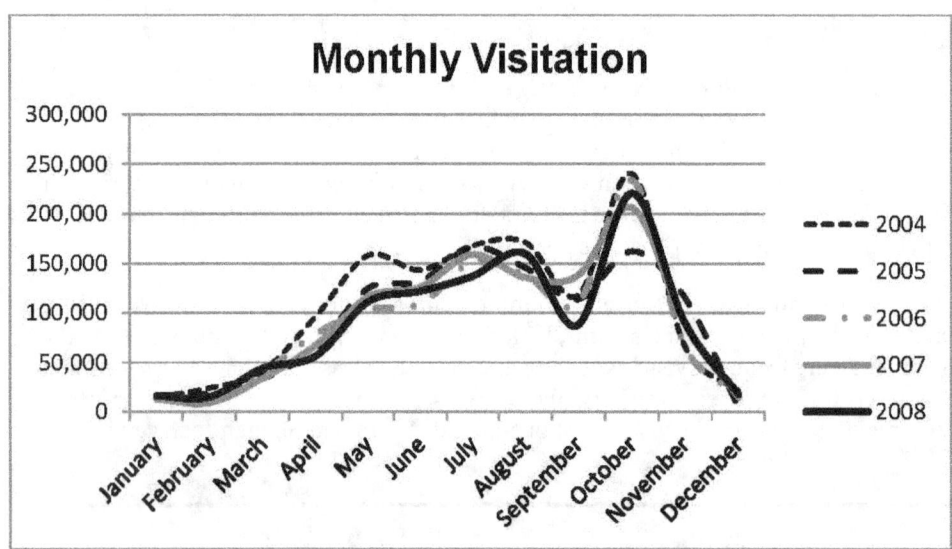

Park Access Routes and Entrance Stations

Vehicles entering the park must pass through one of the four entrance stations to pay an entrance fee for admission to the park. Front Royal, the northernmost entrance, is the most heavily used. I-66 to the north and I-81 to the west are the primary access routes to Shenandoah National Park. Figure 3 shows the location of Shenandoah National Park, the entrance stations, and the key access routes.

Figure 3
Shenandoah National Park and Surrounding Areas
Source: Volpe Center, 2005 Shenandoah Alternative Transportation Study

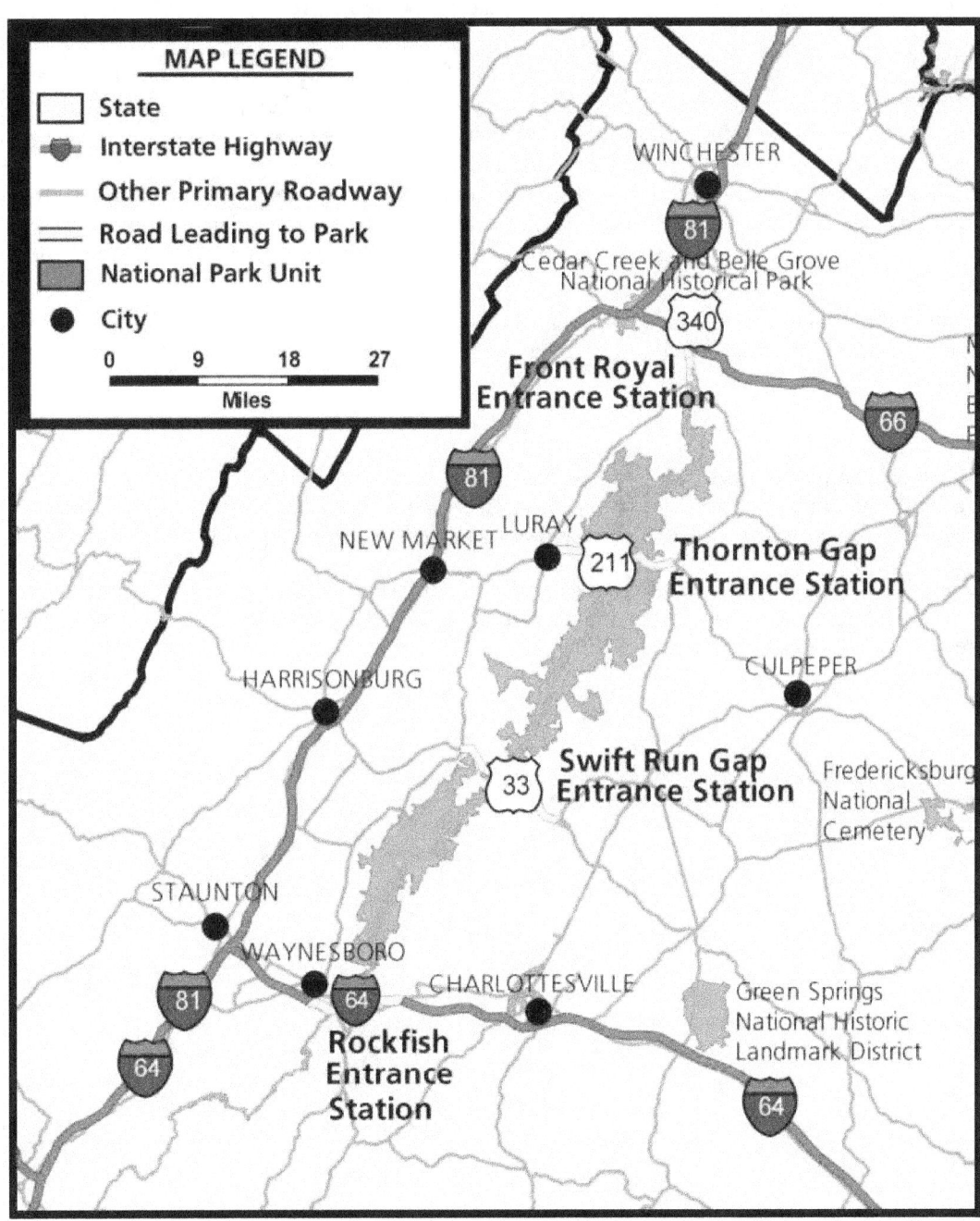

Front Royal

The Front Royal Entrance Station is located about 8 miles southeast of the I-81 / I-66 interchange. It is the most convenient entrance point for travelers arriving from Washington DC. Approximately one-third of all vehicles that arrive at the park enter at the Front Royal Entrance Station. On weekends, additional park staff is on duty in advance of the entrance station to direct pass-holders to one entry gate and to try to answer any questions that will help speed processing. On these days, staff working the entrance gates do not answer questions or provide assistance to arriving visitors, and instead direct all questions to the Dickey Ridge Visitors Center, located about five miles ahead on Skyline Drive.

Thornton Gap

The Thornton Gap Entrance Station is about 31 miles south of the Front Royal entrance. It is located off Route 211, about seven miles east of Luray, Virginia. Approximately 25 percent of park traffic enters through the Thornton Gap entrance. The park headquarters offices are located in the vicinity of this entrance station, but the headquarters offices have few visitor amenities. On peak weekends, the park does provide additional staff to assist with directing traffic through the Thornton Gap entrance.

Swift Run

The Swift Run Entrance Station is located about 34 miles south of the Thornton Gap entrance, off of Route 33 about 20 miles east of Harrisonburg, Virginia. Approximately 20 percent of park traffic enters at the Swift Run entrance.

Rockfish Gap

Rockfish Gap is the southernmost entrance to Shenandoah National Park. It is located about 40 miles south of the Swift Run Entrance Station, between Staunton and Charlottesville, Virginia. Approximately 15 percent of vehicles that arrive at the park enter at the Rockfish Gap Entrance Station.

Approximately five percent of park entries are classified as "boundary entries." These represent trips that enter the park via hiking trailheads located at the park boundary. Figure 4 summarizes monthly visitation by entrance station for calendar year 2009.

Figure 4
Monthly Visitation by Entrance Station (2009)
Source: NPS Public Use Statistics Office

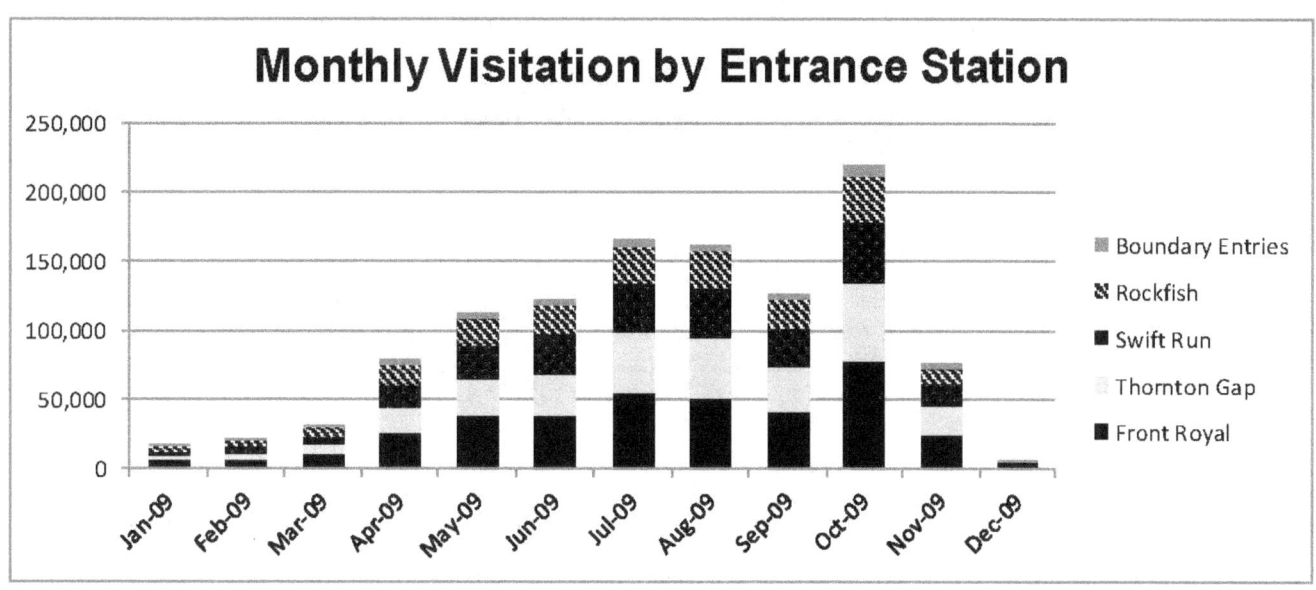

Table 1
Monthly Visitation by Entrance Station (2009)
Source: NPS Public Use Statistics Office

Year	Front Royal	Thornton Gap	Swift Run	Rockfish	Boundary Entries
January	4,548	3,039	3,776	3,072	1,035
February	5,685	4,359	5,404	3,633	1,045
March	9,778	6,460	6,326	5,902	2,602
April	24,737	18,546	16,503	14,385	4,284
May	38,057	26,290	24,267	19,855	4,056
June	37,234	29,568	29,368	21,790	4,461
July	54,357	43,396	35,658	25,973	5,946
August	50,544	43,903	36,630	25,935	4,478
September	40,010	32,274	28,991	20,201	4,782
October	76,453	56,213	45,026	33,522	7,508
November	24,084	20,983	15,845	9,985	4,376
December	962	108	2,318	902	518

Data from the entrance station sales system shows that during October and November the Front Royal entrance station processes 1,000 to 1,500 vehicles per day, and the Thornton Gap entrance station processes 600 to 1,200 vehicles per day. Front Royal typically has about 15 percent more entries than Thornton Gap during this season. The number of entering vehicles at Front Royal and Thornton Gap on select days during a one month period in the Fall of 2009 are shown in Figure 5. The peak arrival time is generally between 11:30 a.m. and 1:00 p.m.

On October 25, 2009, the park experienced extremely high visitation. This was a clear, temperate weekend day at the peak of the foliage changing season. Fees were waived at the Front Royal entrance between 11:30 a.m. and 4:00 p.m. on that day to help alleviate congestion. Over 3,200 vehicles entered at Thornton Gap, and an estimated 3,700 entered at Front Royal.

The sales records indicate that typical practical processing capacity of the Front Royal and Thornton Gap entrance stations is about 60 vehicles per hour per lane; however, the capacity is substantially increased when additional staff are deployed to work the queue of vehicles greeting visitors and answering questions in advance. This reduces the average service time at the entrance stations, and up to 175 vehicles per hour per lane can be processed. By reducing the amount of time spent on visitor questions, entry fee payment type/speed becomes more of a constraining factor.

Figure 5
Daily Entering Vehicles
Source: Shenandoah Entrance Station Sales Records
Note: Chart includes select days when data was available. Blank values indicate that no data was available. Front Royal Entrance Station waived entry fees for several hours on Oct-25 due to congestion. Number below is therefore an estimate of total entries based on typical ratio of Front Royal and Thornton Gap entries.

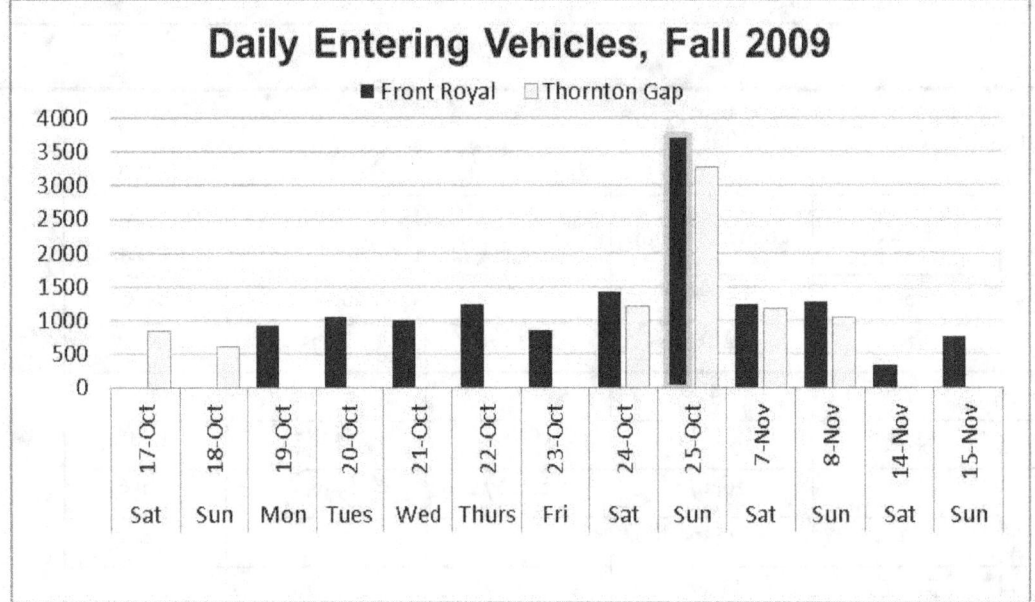

Table 2
Daily Entering Vehicles, Fall 2009
Source: NPS Public Use Statistics Office

Days/Dates	Front Royal	Thornton Gap
Saturday, October 17	NA	839
Sunday, October 18	NA	595
Monday, October 19	915	NA
Tuesday, October 20	1,041	NA
Wednesday, October 21	998	NA
Thursday, October 22	1,225	NA
Friday, October 23	839	NA
Saturday, October 24	1,411	1,199
Sunday, October 25	3,740	3,260
Saturday, November 7	1,240	1,176
Sunday, November 8	1,272	1,036
Saturday, November 14	330	NA
Sunday, November 15	756	NA

Visitors may pay with cash, credit card, or may proceed without paying if they have a valid pass. Staff reported that credit card purchases are slower than cash purchases, though DSL connections installed at Front Royal last year have sped up these transactions at this location. Transaction data do not indicate the service time for individual transactions (transactions are reported by minute only, not by seconds), but the transaction patterns do indicate that credit card processing is significantly slower than cash, and that re-entry processing (for those visitors with a previously purchased pass) is significantly faster than cash. As shown in Figure 6, about 55 percent of visitors pay with cash, 10 percent pay by credit card, and about 35 percent re-enter with a previously purchased pass.

Figure 6
Payment Type, Front Royal and Thornton Gap Entrance Stations
Source: Front Royal Sales Records, October 24-25, 2009

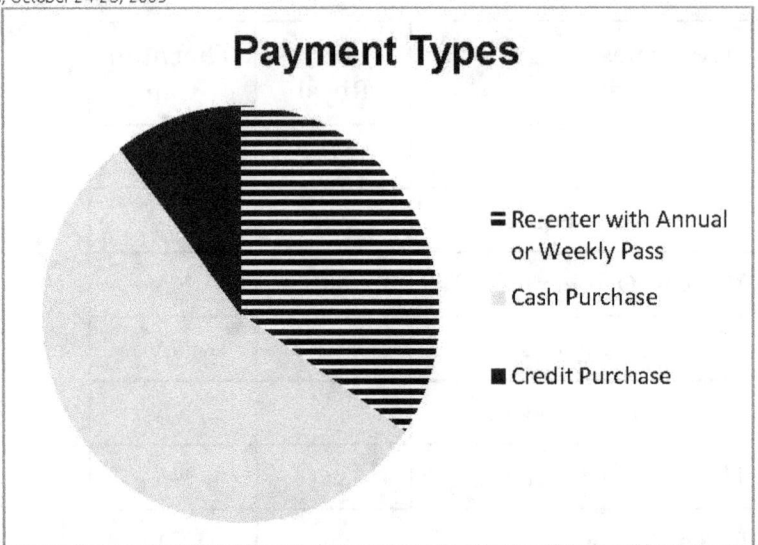

Congestion at Entrance Stations and on Access Routes

Congestion is most problematic at the Front Royal entrance. Anticipating the high demand, additional park staff are on duty at these times to help manage the congestion and move cars through the entrance stations more quickly. However, congestion persists and occasionally stretches back over eight miles to the I-66 interchange. Staff report that congestion issues at Front Royal are problematic most weekend days in October and early November, or about ten to twelve days per year. Also during this time of year, Shenandoah has begun to experience backups on weekdays, and the park is not able to add weekday staff to help manage the increase in traffic.

Front Royal stakeholders indicated that local residents expect the congestion and, while it is inconvenient, they are able to use back roads to avoid extensive delays. Front Royal is working on placing new signage throughout the town to direct some visitor traffic to the town's Main Street, to help generate activity for the local businesses.

Figure 7 below shows the Front Royal entrance station vicinity and highlights the congested area between I-66 the two local access highways and the Shenandoah entrance. Visitors to the park use both routes, with a small majority using Route 55. Staff at the Front Royal chamber of commerce and visitor center confirmed that congestion occurs on these routes.

Figure 7
Congested Approaches to Shenandoah in Front Royal, VA
Source: Volpe Center

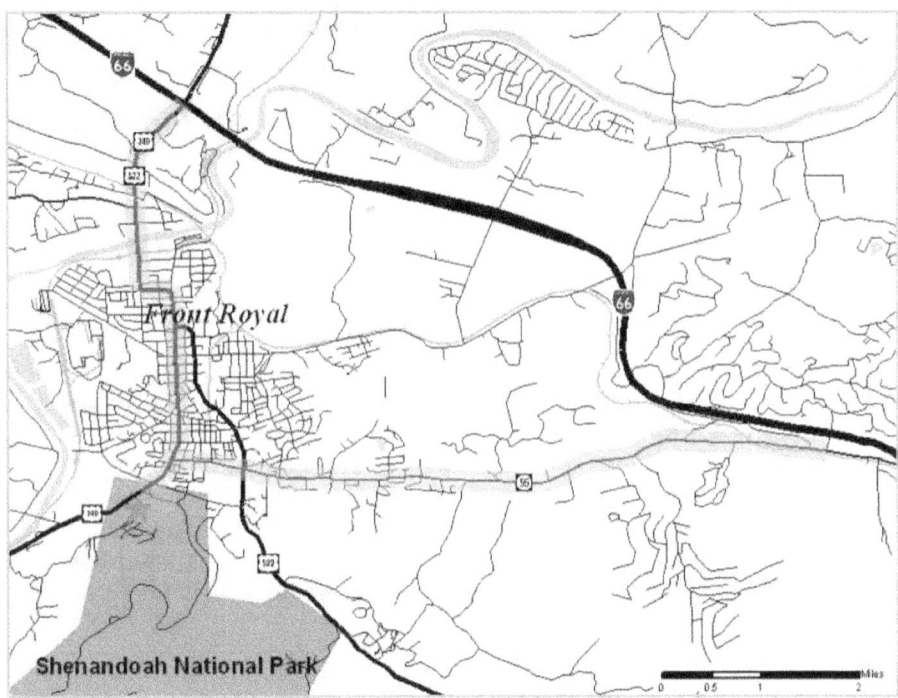

Shenandoah staff reported two potential bottleneck locations in the Front Royal vicinity in addition to the entrance station:

- The intersection of US 340 and Skyline Drive: Drivers arriving from I-66 and the town of Front Royal must make a left-turn onto Skyline Drive. The intersection is unsignalized, and can cause back-ups on US 340 in both directions. On peak days, local law enforcement officers direct traffic at the intersection to help manage traffic flow. Park staff indicated that congestion here is caused by congestion at the Front Royal entrance station. When law enforcement is not available, some of the congestion may be due to the difficulty in southbound traffic crossing northbound traffic to access Skyline Drive.
- Low Gap: Low Gap is an unnamed trailhead parking area about eight miles beyond the Front Royal entrance station. While there are a few parking spaces for visitors to pull off the road, on busy days, these become overcrowded. Park staff report that visitors sometimes park or obstruct traffic on Skyline Drive, causing congestion that can stretch back to the entrance station.

State police, park rangers, and/or park fee program supervisors will sometimes direct entrance station staff to waive entrance fees in order to reduce the congestion. Despite significantly reducing the amount of revenue collected by the park, this tactic does increase throughput at the entrance station and generally helps to relieve the congestion. However, when traffic is blocked at the Low Gap parking area, this does not relieve the congestion. Congestion also occurs occasionally at the Thornton Gap entrance station, but is much less severe.

Currently Highway Advisory Radio (HAR) scripts advise travelers to expect delays at entrance stations during peak times, however, limited broadcast distances often preclude alternative entrance decisions by drivers.

Skyline Drive Closures

Weather-related closures of Skyline Drive generally occur on average ten to fifteen times each winter. The entire length of Skyline Drive may be closed, or it can be closed in sections, and the actual number of closings can vary significantly from year to year. Weather conditions within the park are often much more severe than in surrounding areas because the park is at significantly higher elevation than surrounding areas. It is not uncommon for weather and road conditions in surrounding areas to be clear and safe, while Skyline Drive remains closed because of more severe conditions within the park. Therefore, travelers often do not expect Skyline Drive to be closed (especially when the portion of the drive that is visible to the public is clear), and they arrive at the entrance gates to find that the road is closed, leading to unnecessary travel and frustration. In some cases, this may lead to verbal abuse directed at the fee collectors. The park has taken measures to reduce visitor frustration by posting photographs at the entrance that show conditions at higher elevations.

The procedures for closing and re-opening Skyline Drive are described in the park's 2009 Winter Operations Plan. The notification sequence for Skyline Drive closures and re-openings is shown in Figure 8, below. Decisions about closing and re-opening Skyline Drive are the responsibility of park Law Enforcement Rangers. When a decision is made to change the status of Skyline Drive, a ranger will notify the Shenandoah Park Public Safety and Communication Center (Communication Center). The staff person on duty then has a series of responsibilities including assisting park staff and rangers in evacuating or relocating staff and visitors as appropriate; notifying all park staff via two-way radio, email and an employee phone system; updating the general park phone system; updating the park website with closure information; and handling phone calls. The Communication Center is staffed 24 hours a day, 7 days per week, generally with one staff person at any time.

Figure 8
Notification Sequence for Skyline Drive Closures and Re-openings
*Opening decisions made in consultation with Maintenance Road Supervisor

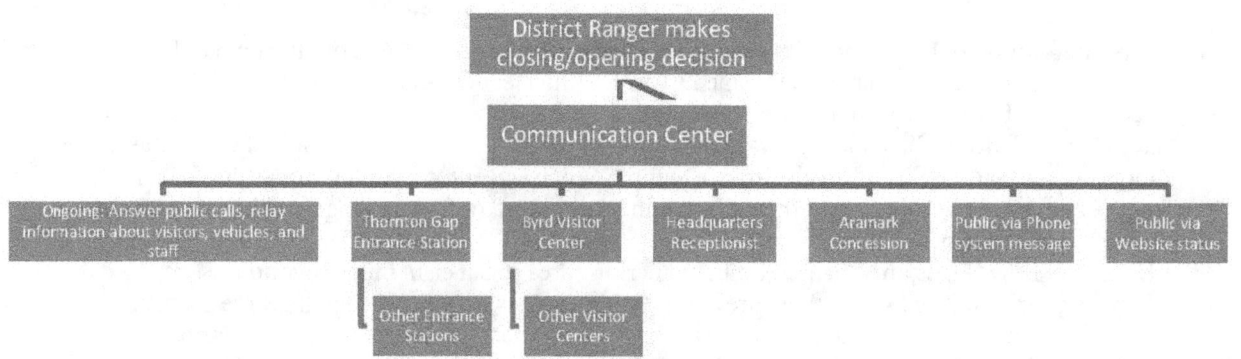

Existing Traveler Information Systems

Shenandoah National Park provides travel information – entrance locations, travel directions, weather conditions, and operating hours – to prospective visitors in several ways: on the park's web site, through the park phone system, and using park-operated highway advisory radio (HAR). Currently no information is provided about congestion or alternate route options. In addition, all of the information systems require travelers to anticipate adverse conditions within the park and seek out the information. The components of the existing Traveler Information System at Shenandoah National Park are summarized in this section; readers are referred to the 2005 Shenandoah Alternative Transportation Planning Study for additional information about each of the existing traveler information systems.

Park Phone System (540-999-3500)

The park phone system provides extensive information about the park through an automated phone tree. The main phone number, listed on the park website and brochures, offers a menu of options including weather report and road conditions. The park's phone system was updated in 2008 to a voice-over-IP unified call manager system provided by Verizon and Cisco Systems. The new system offers more voicemail functions for staff and can handle more simultaneous calls than the previous system. Phone system messages can be recorded from any location, using password access. The system can manage scheduled announcements, and can store up to six pre-recorded greetings on each extension. Currently, there is no way of monitoring the number of calls to the phone system.

The main welcome message that all callers hear when dialing the number listed above refers callers to the Shenandoah website and lists a menu of options for callers to hear more information about the following topics:

- Park facilities and Skyline drive status
- Camping
- Lodging
- General information, including park activities and ranger programs
- Park business offices, job information, and contact individual employees
- To reach an operator during business hours

The main welcome message is updated as needed by the Public Affairs office. It is not updated during events.

If callers press "1" to find out the status of Skyline Drive, they are directed to a second menu consisting of the following options:

- Road and weather condition information
- Basic park facility information
- Ranger program and activity information and contact Byrd Visitor Center staff

Communication Center staff record the road and weather condition message several times per day during emergency events when the status of Skyline Drive changes. Congestion information is not provided.

Park staff reported that updating phone system messages can be a quick process (no more than five minutes) if it can be completed without interruption. Communication Center staff reported that because they are frequently interrupted – by incoming phone calls from travelers, rangers, and other park staff – updating the recorded message for the phone system becomes more time intensive. A single update can take 30 to 45 minutes if the staff person is interrupted several times while trying to record the updated message. Park staff noted that people (usually park concessionaire and park staff) calling in to the phone system often request to speak with an operator to verify that the message is accurate. These requests are directed to the Communication Center staff person, adding to their responsibilities during events. Updating the phone system during road closure events uses a significant portion of Communication Center staff resources.

Park Website (www.nps.gov/shen/home.htm)

The park website, hosted by the National Park Service, provides information on opening and closing dates, available facilities and services, fees, and activities. Most updates to the website are managed by the

Interpretation Division. In 2008, the park began providing notices regarding the status of Skyline Drive on its website, shown in Figure 9 and available at http://www.nps.gov/shen/planyourvisit/drive_status.htm. The Interpretation Division created a fairly simple web interface for the Communication Center staff person to maintain. Communication Center staff are responsible for updating that information at least once per day during closures.*

Currently, updating the park phone system takes priority over updating the park website during events. The phone system is generally updated several times per day during a weather event, while the website may only be updated once per day.

Figure 9
Skyline Drive Status Page on the Shenandoah National Park Website

---

* Park staff find that recent updates to website management software have resulted in reduced reliability for posting real-time info. Updates may take hours, days, or weeks to appear (or not show up at all) on the public site. Until this problem is resolved, utilizing the website to disseminate real-time information is not considered a viable option. This works against the fact that an increasing number of visitors have access to web-enabled mobile phones.

Press Releases

The park Public Affairs office releases seasonal and event notices to press outlets. The press releases include general advisory notices about road construction and scheduled closings, but are not typically issued during events. The park currently issues a press release at the beginning of the winter season to remind the public that Skyline Drive closes several times during the winter.

Twitter

The Public Affairs office is starting to explore new media such as blogs and Twitter to circulate information. Shenandoah began broadcasting on Twitter in 2009 (using the handle ShenandoahNPS) and the account has nearly 500 followers. Throughout the 2009/2010 winter 14 messages were posted relating to the status of Skyline Drive. There is no official procedure for posting Skyline Drive status on Twitter.

Highway Advisory Radio

Broadcast stations with a two to three mile range are located at the Front Royal and Rockfish Gap entrance stations. Broadcast messages are played on a continuous loop, and are recorded four to six times per year by entrance station staff. The broadcasts are not updated during events.

Note that since the 2005 assessment was completed, the Highway Advisory Radio (HAR) broadcast capability at the Thornton Gap Entrance Station was lost. Functional HAR broadcast stations are still in use at the Front Royal and Rockfish Gap Entrance Stations. There are no current plans to restore the Thornton Gap broadcast capability.

Official Maps and Guides

Available at park facilities, chambers of commerce, and area visitor centers, Park brochures and trail maps provide general park information and show major points of interest. These maps and guides are generally updated every one to three years by the park Interpretation Division. They do not currently provide seasonal information or advisories.

Park Visitor Guide

The Overlook Visitor Guide is provided to all visitors at the entrance stations during spring, summer, and fall. It is produced two times per year by the Interpretation Division, and includes seasonal information and notices.

Road Signs

Brown recreational guide signs throughout the region provide direction and distance information related to the park. All of the park signs are static signs; the park does not own or operate any variable message signs (VMS) at this time. Signs are replaced as needed by park facilities and Virginia Department of Transportation staff. The locations of signs directing travelers to Shenandoah National Park are shown in Figure 10 below.

**Figure 10
Shenandoah National Park Signs**
Source: Shenandoah Facilities Division Sign Inventory

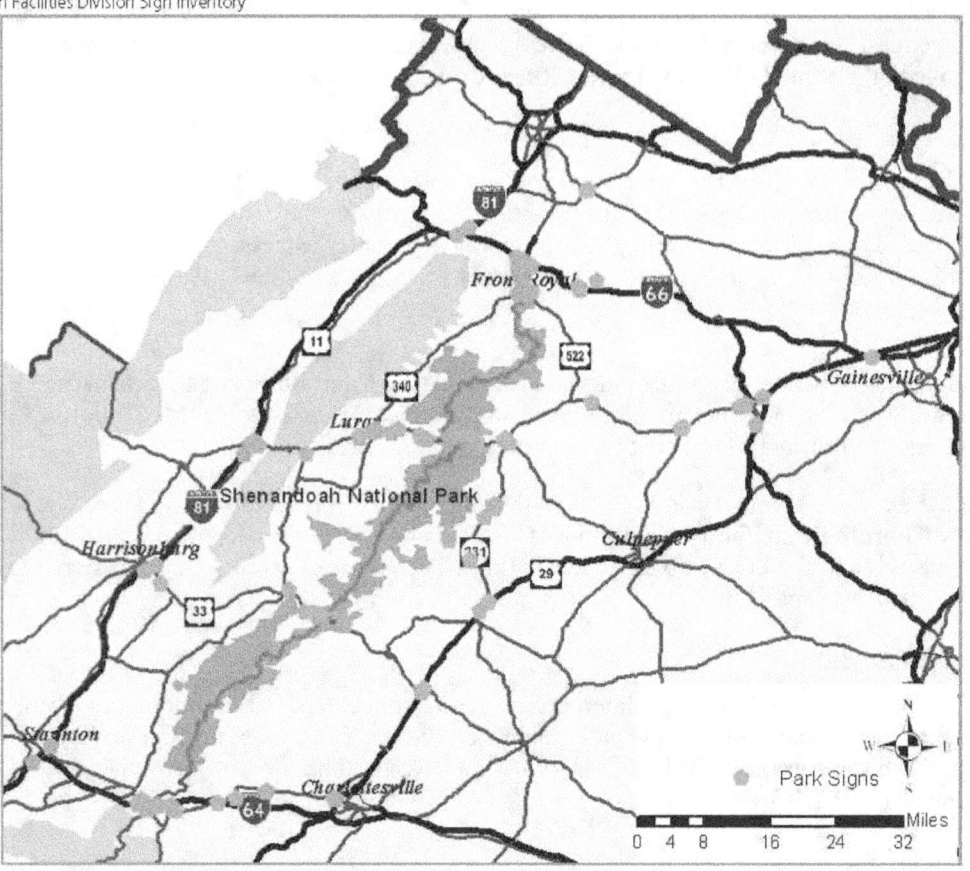

Park traveler information is also produced and distributed by agencies and organizations other than the park. These outside information sources include:

- Concessioner maps and guides,
- Local visitors bureaus,
- Local chambers of commerce,
- Travel websites (e.g., tripadvisor.com), and
- Local radio stations.

These outside information sources provide general travel information related to the park, but with the exception of hiking-related conditions provided by the Potomac Appalachian Trail Club, none currently provide updates during congestion or weather-related events.

Evaluation of Strategies

This section describes and evaluates several possible options for improving traveler information regarding Skyline Drive closures and addressing congestion at Park entrances.

Improved Traveler Information Regarding Skyline Drive Closures

Based on the review of weather-related closures of Skyline Drive and existing traveler information systems, the following possible improvements for disseminating news of closures and re-openings to travelers were identified:

- Modify Use of Existing Traveler Information Systems
- Participate in VDOT 511 Traveler Information System
- Install Variable Message Signs

Each of these options is described and evaluated below.

Modify Use of Existing Traveler Information Systems

The phone system, website, and Twitter posts are useful traveler information systems for winter road closures. However, because park weather conditions are often quite different than surrounding conditions, a more visible traveler information system that alerts travelers to the road closures even when they do not seek out the information would be more effective for disseminating information about weather-related events. The park could improve the traveler information provided through these systems as follows:

Phone System

- During events, provide a brief message about the status of Skyline Drive as part of the welcome message on the phone system.
- Use standard pre-recorded messages to reduce the time required to update the phone system.
- Include a time stamp as part of all event updates.

Website

- More frequent updates during road closure events.

Twitter

- Integrate the use of Twitter into the emergency operations procedures. These quick updates could become a valuable resource for disseminating event information.
- Automatic Twitter messages linked to Skyline Drive status updates on the park website.

All of these changes could be implemented at no capital cost; however, they would require dedication of some staff time. Staff capacity is an important limitation during road closure events. Responsibilities related to staff and visitor safety, as well as internal communication about reporting duties and conditions are prioritized above public traveler information. Dedication of staff time to traveler information must be managed carefully. The park does not currently track how many people visit this webpage or how many people call in to the phone system during the winter season. These data would support a decision to prioritize the system that is used most frequently.

Including Skyline Drive closures as part of the welcome message on the phone system would make the information more accessible to callers, and could alert people calling for other reasons (operating hours, activities, etc.) to closures that they otherwise would not anticipate. It would, however, add a new task to event procedures. If uninterrupted, recording the message would take only about five minutes, but with many interruptions, it could take much longer.

Use of pre-recorded messages for Skyline Drive closures could reduce the staff time required to update the messages with closure information. The phone system can store up to six pre-recorded messages for each mailbox. These messages can be selected either based on a pre-set schedule or manually. The schedule option probably would not be useful for managing events, but manually selecting a pre-recorded message rather than recording a new message each time could streamline the process. Skyline Drive is often closed and re-opened in sections, thus more than six message options are needed to cover all possible closures situations, but pre-recorded messages could be used for the most frequent situations.

Updating the status of Skyline Drive on the park website should be able to happen very quickly. Currently these updates are a low priority and are generally updated just once per day during events. Without knowing how many people are accessing this information and recognizing current software limitations experienced by the park, it is difficult to prioritize it. However, if this system was prioritized and became the best source for reliable event information, it could reduce reliance on the phone system, which is more labor intensive. The web updates could also be tied to text message, email or twitter messages that would help disseminate the information more broadly.

Use of Twitter is growing rapidly, though it is still used by only a segment of potential Shenandoah travelers. Twitter has an advantage over other existing traveler information systems in that it requires less effort by the traveler to access the information. Anyone using Twitter who follows the Shenandoah feed or searches anything related to Shenandoah on a computer or mobile device is likely to come across posts about Skyline Drive closures. The initial success of the Shenandoah Twitter account – nearly 500 followers – indicates that there is a market for this information. Including Twitter updates in Shenandoah's event procedures could bolster the quality and consistency of information.

Twitter messages can be automatically generated to broadcast messages related to website updates. North Carolina Department of Transportation has developed such a system as part of its incident management procedures.

Participate in 511 Virginia Traveler Information System

The Virginia Department of Transportation (VDOT) statewide traveler information service, 511 Virginia, collects information on traffic incidents, construction, weather forecasts, transit, and tourism information from partner agencies throughout the state and provides travelers with free and continuous information via an automated phone system (by calling the number 5-1-1), website, cable television, and variable message signs posted throughout the state. Travelers can receive personalized information feeds from the 511 system via e-mail or text message. 511 systems have been supported by the USDOT for the last ten years, and traveler awareness and use of 511 systems is expanding in Virginia and throughout the US.

VDOT accepts travel-related information through the Northwestern Traffic Operations Center, generally by phone (1-866-597-1851). The Traffic Operations Center staff forward the information to disseminate it as they see appropriate. The VDOT 511 Project Manager indicated that most likely, information about Skyline Drive closures would be used to generate a "floodgate message" on the 511 phone service. This message would be played to any caller requesting travel information for the county in which the closure occurs, or specifically requesting information about Skyline Drive, Route 211, or Route 340.

To participate in the 511 system, specific communication procedures and standard message content should be agreed upon in advance to ensure consistency and to reduce staff time required to display variable messages.

The 511 Virginia system is advertised throughout the state, and is probably more widely known than the Shenandoah phone system and website. Since its inception in 2002, 511 Virginia has received more than 5.2

million calls and 2 million web site visits. In addition, the 511 system is maintained off-site and off-server, which offers some benefits in terms of maintenance responsibility, cost and redundancy.

The personalization features of the 511 Virginia system offer some benefits over Shenandoah's internal systems, primarily by allowing frequent travelers to get automatic email or text message notices about travel conditions in the park. However, fewer than ten percent of Shenandoah visitors visit the park frequently and only about a quarter of the park's visitors are Virginia residents. Most park visitors would still need to anticipate potential closures or adverse conditions and check the 511 website or call the 511 number.

Install Variable Message Signs

Shenandoah may be able to display messages on VMS if it purchased and installed new VMS in locations targeted to Shenandoah travelers. These could be new signs, or variable message signboards added to some of the existing static signs that direct travelers to the park.

Purchasing VMS could give the park greater ability to notify travelers of Skyline Drive closures if VDOT supported the sign content and operation. VDOT and the park would need to reach agreement about the design, message content, and operation in order to install VMS boards on signs on state roadways (any numbered route in the vicinity).

VMS are an attractive traveler information system because they provide timely information to all travelers, and require no effort by the traveler to receive the information.

VDOT's Variable Message Signs (VMS) are managed through the 511 Virginia system, and their use is governed by VDOT's Changeable Message Sign Procedure, published in February 2004. The VDOT Changeable Message Sign Procedure indicates that VDOT personnel manage the operations of any VMS on a state owned road; Park staff would not be able to control the signs directly even if the park purchased the signs exclusively for Park-related traveler information. Permission from VDOT to install any new VMS on state-owned roads is required.

The Changeable Message Sign Procedure lists several authorized purposes for the use of VMS:

- Displaying messages about an unexpected situation that reduces roadway capacity on an adjoining route could be an authorized cause for displaying a VMS message, depending on the location, severity, and duration of the situation.
- Alleviating major traffic problems generated by special events or advising drivers of adverse traffic conditions created as a result of a special event.

VDOT staff have discretion in interpreting whether a particular message is admissible under the purposes listed in the Procedure. A VDOT 511 Project Manager indicated that notices about Skyline Drive closures probably would not warrant display on VDOT's existing VMS. VDOT currently has VMS on Interstate-66 and Interstate-81 where Shenandoah-bound traffic makes up a small portion of the total traffic passing by these signs.

It may be feasible for Skyline Drive closure information to be displayed on portable VMS or new permanent roadside VMS on the routes approaching park entrances, such as Routes 55 and 340 near Front Royal, Route 211 near Thornton Gap, Route 33 near Swift Run Gap, and/or Route 250 near Rockfish Gap. While these are also state routes governed by VDOT procedures, the total traffic volumes on these routes is lower and is more likely to be impacted by Shenandoah National Park closures.

Several preliminary options for VMS that may effectively communicate information about Skyline Drive closures to travelers at an appropriate scale and complexity are shown in Figure 11. The first option could provide full event information, while the others would provide limited information and rely on a secondary information source such as 511 Virginia or the park phone system to provide more extensive information. The cost of a completely new VMS would vary significantly depending on size and message content, but could cost on the order of $5,000 to $30,000 plus annual operations and maintenance costs.

Seasonal use of VDOTs portable VMS is also an option that could be discussed with VDOT staff. A 2004 VDOT VMS inventory reported 30 portable VMS owned by the Staunton and Culpepper Districts of VDOT.

Figure 11
Example Variable Message Sign Options

Full Matrix LED Add-on	Open/Closed LED Add-on	Flashing Beacon Add-on
Operator Interface: Dial-up or leased-line circuit	Operator Interface: Telephone Paging System	Operator Interface: Telephone Paging System
Power Supply: Service connection	Power Supply: Solar + Battery	Power Supply: Solar + Battery
Estimated Cost: $10,000-$15,000 per sign plus operations/maintenance	Estimated Cost: $5,000-$8,000 per sign plus operations/maintenance	Estimated Cost: $5,000-$8,000 per sign* plus operations/maintenance

Many issues would need to be addressed before any of these options could be implemented, including:

- Permitting: Coordination with VDOT would be needed to determine appropriate sign design and messaging in order to gain permission for any VMS use on nearby state routes.
- Power: Depending on the sign type and location, a hardwired power connection may be needed or a solar battery design may be sufficient.
- Communication: The sign would need to be connected to the VDOT operations center, probably through a telephone paging system or a dial-up internet connection where available. Establishing credible, reliable communication procedures for delivering information about closures and re-openings would be essential.
- Standard Operating Procedures: Standard messages would need to be created, and responsibility for activating and de-activating the messages would need to be defined.
- Funding: A source of funding for both upfront costs as well as operating and maintenance expenses would need to be identified.
- Maintenance: Typically VDOT performs maintenance on signs within its right-of-way. Shenandoah would most likely be responsible for paying for maintenance and replacement costs. Prior to installing signs, VDOT and Shenandoah should determine how the condition of signs will be monitored.

Addressing Congestion at Park Entrances

Based on the review of access to Shenandoah National Park and congestion at the Front Royal entrance station, several possible improvements have been identified. The possible improvements include strategies for improving traveler information about the congestion, as well as strategies for increasing the processing capacity at the Front Royal entrance station. Temporary measures are especially critical during fall foliage peaks in mid- to late October

Provide Congestion Information
- Provide high profile, seasonal messages about congestion on the park website and phone system.
- Use portable VMS in Front Royal and static road signs along US 522 to encourage visitors to enter through Thornton Gap when capacity at Front Royal is exceeded.

Increase Entrance Station Capacity and/or Queue Storage
- Formalize a procedure for waiving entrance fees when congestion becomes problematic.
- Install tandem entrance booths.
- Re-direct exiting traffic and allow entering traffic to use both sides of the roadway as shown in Figure 14.
- Widen the Front Royal entrance to provide additional entrance lanes and booths.
- Provide more storage for queued vehicles.

Discount Early and/or Late Arrivals on Peak Visitation Days

Each of these options is described and evaluated below.

Provide Congestion Information

Alerting travelers to the potential for delays at the Front Royal Entrance station may reduce visitor frustration and may encourage some travelers to shift their travel plans in a way that eases the congestion.

Provide seasonal messages about congestion on the park website and phone system.

Notices on the park website and phone system about peak travel times and expected delays may help travelers anticipate congestion and plan accordingly.

If visitors are aware of the potential for delay, they may decide to use an alternate entrance to the park, and some travelers may decide to arrive earlier or later to avoid congestion (peak-spreading). Providing advanced information about entrance station congestion may reduce visitor frustration simply by providing a warning and also by encouraging peak-spreading. However, many travelers would not receive these messages if they did not call the park or visit the park website before their visit.

Use Portable VMS to Suggest Entering through Thornton Gap

On peak days, traffic entering Front Royal is about 15 percent higher than at Thornton Gap. While data indicating visitor travel patterns within the park is not available, park staff suggested that many day-use visitors make a one-way loop through the park. Encouraging some visitors to reverse the direction of the loop to enter through Thornton Gap and exit through Front Royal, as shown in Figure 12, would better utilize the entrance station and Skyline Drive capacity, and would add minimal additional travel time.

Portable VMS could be used to suggest an alternate route to the Thornton Gap entrance station. The VMS could be placed in the town of Front Royal along US 55 and US 340 alerting Shenandoah travelers to extensive congestion on southbound Skyline Drive, and advising them to use US 522 south to enter the park on US 211 at Thornton Gap. Although this is an extensive detour– about 25 miles –US 522 between Front Royal and Thornton Gap is a fairly simple, direct route to the Thornton Gap entrance, and if visitors would simply be reversing the direction of the loop they plan to make, it would not add to their travel time. Static signs indicating the path to Thornton Gap along the detour route would help assure re-routed visitors that they were headed in the right direction. Currently there are no Shenandoah signs along this stretch of US 522. Proposed locations for three portable VMS in Front Royal and three static road signs along US 522 are shown in Figure 12, indicated by orange boxes.

Figure 12
Proposed Alternate Route and Sign Locations
Source: Google Maps

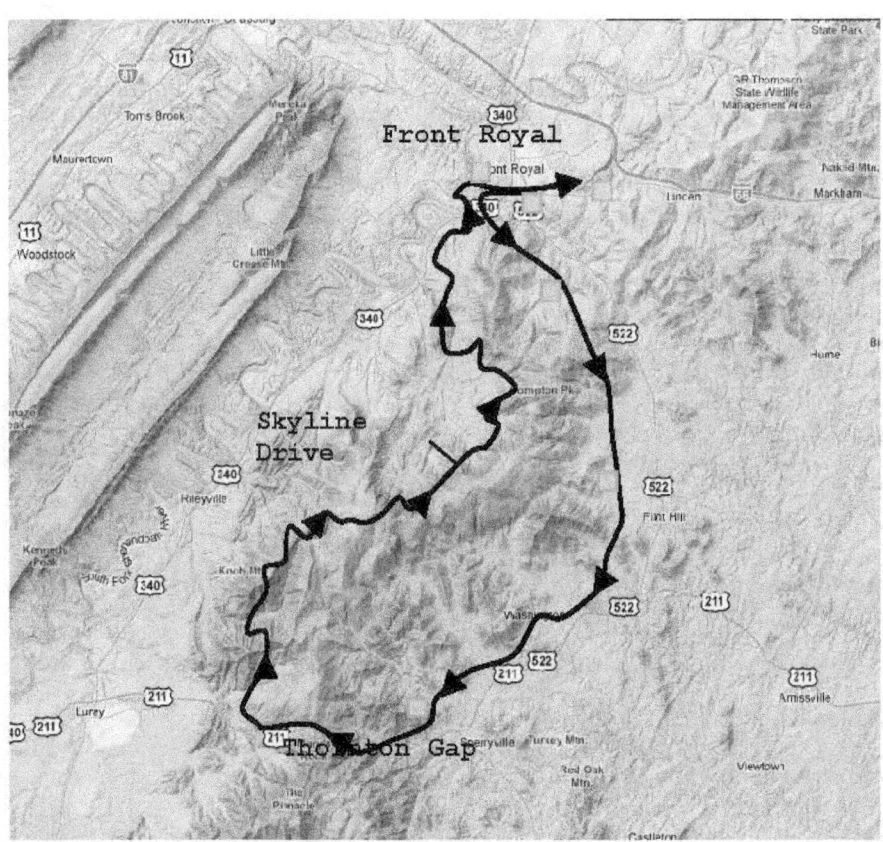

Staff reported that the Thornton Gap entrance station occasionally experiences congestion, however it is not as severe or frequent as the congestion experienced at Front Royal. Entrance station data from October 2009 show that Thornton Gap processed about 15 percent fewer vehicles than Front Royal on peak days. Thornton Gap and Front Royal both have three entrance lanes and should be able to achieve comparable processing capacity. Shifting five to ten percent of arriving vehicles from the Front Royal entrance to the Thornton Gap entrance would help balance the congestion.

The effectiveness of voluntary re-routing would depend on the effectiveness of the signage plan and on possible changes in visitor behavior and travel patterns (as described above, visitors could reserve the direction of their travel plans, entering at Thornton Gap rather than Front Royal). Additional staff may be needed to assist processing at Thornton Gap, as they are at Front Royal, if a significant number of visitors shifted to using the Thornton Gap entrance.

As described above, permission from and coordination with VDOT would be needed to prepare appropriate message content, establish management and funding agreements, and to ensure adequate communication between VDOT, local law enforcement, and park staff to use portable VMS on these routes, consistent with the VDOT CMS Procedure. It seems reasonable that VDOT would be willing to authorize this use of portable VMS under the special event purpose authorized in the CMS Procedure. Coordination with the town of Front Royal would also be necessary.

Portable VMS cost about $20,000, however it is possible these may be borrowed or rented from VDOT or a third party. As of 2004, the VDOT Staunton district had about 15 portable VMS according to the statewide Amber Alert plan. Standard static signs cost about $1,000 each.

Increase Front Royal Capacity and/or Queue Storage

Park staff reported that the entrance gate is the primary cause of congestion in Front Royal. Increasing throughput capacity of the entrance gate, then, should reduce the congestion. There are several options for increasing peak capacity at the Front Royal Entrance Station. A closer evaluation of entrance gate operations and capacity upstream and downstream of the gate is needed to fully evaluate these options.

Formalize a procedure for waiving entrance fees when congestion becomes problematic.

The park currently does this when directed by local law enforcement, Fee Supervisors, and Law Enforcement Rangers. This relieves the congestion temporarily unless Skyline Drive is blocked at the Low Gap. This option is fairly effective, but requires that the park forego revenue that is needed to fund visitor facility improvement projects thoroughout the park. On October 25, 2009 when the park waived entry fees for approximately four hours, an estimated $15,000 to $20,000 of revenue was forgone.

While it is not the most desirable solution, it is only necessary a few hours per year and helps to maintain a safer and more pleasant visitor experience. Creating a more proactive procedure for when and for how long to waive entrance fees could help keep the queue to a reasonable level without foregoing any more revenue than necessary. A closer review of the congestion pattern would be needed to determine appropriate trigger points and durations for waiving fees.

Install tandem entrance booths.

Tandem entrance booths would operate similar to many gas stations, with two places in a single lane where a vehicle could be serviced. The increase in capacity would not be as great as adding additional entrance lanes because the second booth would sometimes be blocked by a vehicle at the first booth. There are no known National Park examples of this design, though it is used successfully to increase capacity at some Toll Plazas. The main advantage of this approach is that it would increase capacity without requiring roadway expansion or foregoing fees.

Re-direct exiting traffic and allow entering traffic to use both sides of the roadway.

It does not appear that the road approaching the entrance station is wide enough to accommodate an additional lane (for example, by re-striping or using shoulders) without widening the road.

There is over 3,200 feet of storage for vehicles approaching the Front Royal entrance stations on Park land. Nearly all of this distance is single-lane roadway. A short existing road between the entrance station and US 340 that connects Skyline Drive and East Criser Road could possibly be used for exiting vehicles, so that both sides of the road could be used for entering queue storage. This would create an additional 2,000 feet of storage for entering vehicles. This traffic pattern is illustrated in Figure 14.

Creating this additional storage area would not reduce the delay for visitors, but would help reduce the traffic impacts on the Town.

Figure 14
Front Royal Entrance Station Possible Queue Storage Option
Source: Google Maps

Widen Entrance

Widening the Front Royal entrance to add an additional entry lane and booth would significantly increase capacity and could improve traffic flow and safety. It would be costly, create some environmental impacts, and would require additional staffing to man the additional booth. Park staff reported that there are steep grades on either side of the entrance station, which would make widening expensive and could be prohibitive. Figure 15 shows that the existing shoulders are quite narrow, so that paving and grading would likely be needed to widen the entrance.

Discount Early and/or Late Arrivals on Peak Visitation Days

Providing discounts to visitors arriving early or late would spread arrivals and help alleviate congestion. There are no known examples of National Parks that use variable pricing throughout the day to manage demand. Changes in fee policy must be consistent with NPS fee program policy.

Figure 15
Front Royal Entrance Station
Source: Google Maps

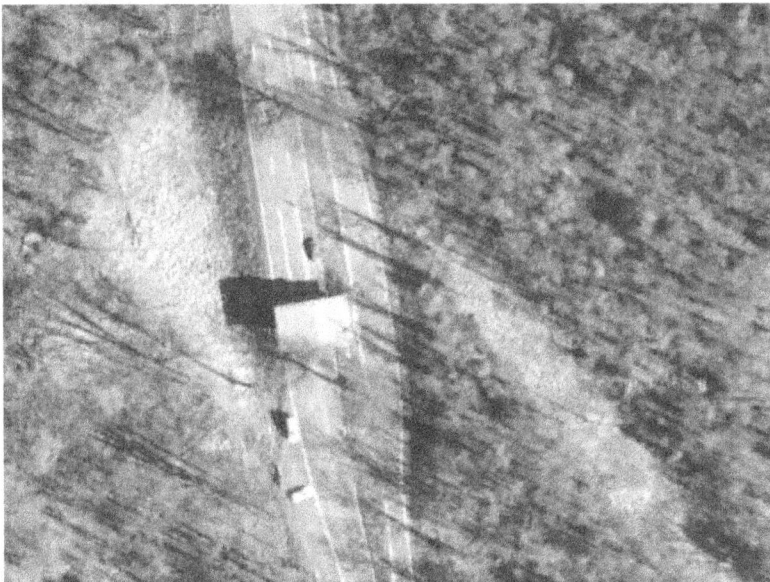

Recommended Actions

Based on this review of Shenandoah National Park's traveler information systems, congestion events and weather-related closures, the following actions are recommended.

Recommended Actions		Event Type	
		Closure	Congestion
1. Participate in 511 Virginia system			
Description	Establish communication procedure for providing information to VDOT Regional Operations Center for posting to the Virginia 511 system and prepare template messages for consistent information sharing.	X	X
Leader	SHEN headquarters		
Participants	VDOT Regional Ops. Staff, SHEN Communication Center		
2. Pursue use of permanent or portable VMS to display closure and/or congestion event information on key SHEN access routes.			
Description	<ul><li>Determine whether VDOT and Town of Front Royal would permit VMS such as those shown in Figure 11 to be used on: - VA 55 and/or 340 in Front Royal -VA 211 near Thornton Gap -VA 33 near Swift Run Gap, and/or -VA 250 near Rockfish Gap.</li><li>Determine whether portable VMS could be rented from VDOT or others.</li><li>Address issues listed on pages 17 and 18 before purchasing or installing VMS.</li></ul>	X	X
Leader	SHEN headquarters		
Participants	VDOT Regional Ops. Staff, Front Royal Public Works		
3. Provide congestion information through SHEN website and phone system.			
Description	<ul><li>Post prominent notices on the park website and phone system throughout the fall season alerting travelers to the potential for delays at the Front Royal entrance station at peak times to help travelers anticipate congestion and plan accordingly.</li><li>Encourage visitors who will make a loop through the park to enter through Thornton Gap and exit through Front Royal.</li></ul>		X
Leader	SHEN Interpretation Division (web); Public Affairs Office (phone)		
Participants	SHEN Superintendent's office		
4. Update Shenandoah procedures for disseminating information during Skyline Drive closures.			
Description	<ul><li>Add 511 communication procedures, prioritize website updates, formalize use of Twitter, include Skyline Drive status as part of the phone system welcome message during the winter. (See Figure 16)</li><li>Record and store template messages for the Road Weather mailbox of the phone system describing Skyline Drive statuses that can be selected when closures occur.</li><li>Consider shifting responsibility for phone system updates down the communication tree to help manage communication center responsibilities. Phone system can be updated from remote locations.</li></ul>	X	
Leader	SHEN headquarters		
Participants	SHEN Communication Center		

Figure 16
Proposed Notification Sequence for Skyline Drive Closures and Re-openings
*Opening decisions made in consultation with Maintenance Road Supervisor

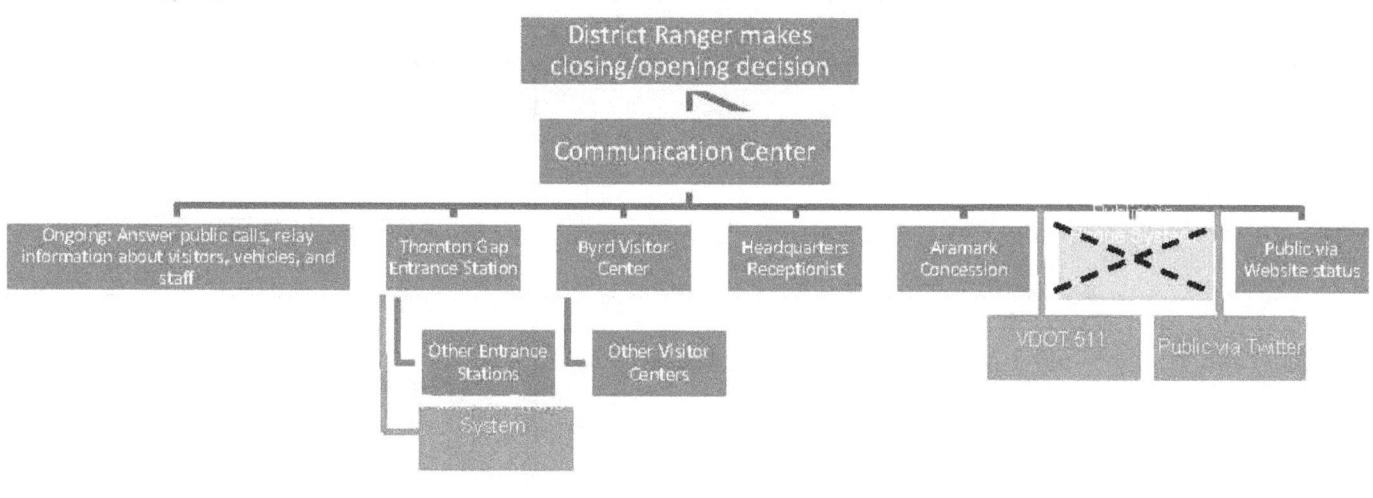

REPORT DOCUMENTATION PAGE		*Form Approved* *OMB No. 0704-0188*

The public reporting burden for this collection of information is estimated to average 1 hour per response, including the time for reviewing instructions, searching existing data sources, gathering and maintaining the data needed, and completing and reviewing the collection of information. Send comments regarding this burden estimate or any other aspect of this collection of information, including suggestions for reducing the burden, to Department of Defense, Washington Headquarters Services, Directorate for Information Operations and Reports (0704-0188), 1215 Jefferson Davis Highway, Suite 1204, Arlington, VA 22202-4302. Respondents should be aware that notwithstanding any other provision of law, no person shall be subject to any penalty for failing to comply with a collection of information if it does not display a currently valid OMB control number.
PLEASE DO NOT RETURN YOUR FORM TO THE ABOVE ADDRESS.

1. REPORT DATE *(DD-MM-YYYY)* August 2011	2. REPORT TYPE Final	3. DATES COVERED *(From - To)* Sep 2009 - Aug 2011
4. TITLE AND SUBTITLE Shenandoah National Park Traveler Information Coordination Study		5a. CONTRACT NUMBER F4505087777 Amendment 1
		5b. GRANT NUMBER
		5c. PROGRAM ELEMENT NUMBER
6. AUTHOR(S) Kenneth Miller Kathleen Sylvester		5d. PROJECT NUMBER PMIS No. 145352
		5e. TASK NUMBER NP61
		5f. WORK UNIT NUMBER
7. PERFORMING ORGANIZATION NAME(S) AND ADDRESS(ES) U.S. Department of Transportation Research and Innovative Transportation Administration John A. Volpe National Transportation Systems Center 55 Broadway, Cambridge, MA 02142		8. PERFORMING ORGANIZATION REPORT NUMBER DOT-VNTSC-NPS-11-22
9. SPONSORING/MONITORING AGENCY NAME(S) AND ADDRESS(ES) U.S. Department of the Interior National Park Service Northeast Region 15 State Street, Boston, MA 02109		10. SPONSOR/MONITOR'S ACRONYM(S) NPS NER & SHEN
		11. SPONSOR/MONITOR'S REPORT NUMBER(S) 134/110081

12. DISTRIBUTION/AVAILABILITY STATEMENT
Public distribution/availability

13. SUPPLEMENTARY NOTES

14. ABSTRACT
Shenandoah National Park is located in northwestern Virginia, about 60 miles southwest of Washington, DC. The Front Royal Entrance Station is located about 8 miles southeast of the I-81 / I-66 interchange, where approximately 1/3 of visitors enter the park. This report focuses on identifying transportation information solutions to alert visitors approaching Shenandoah from the vicinity of Front Royal about potential park closures due to weather and congestions issues. With the current traveler information systems, most visitors don't find out about closures until they arrive at the park and it is difficult to alert visitors to alternative routes when congestion occurs, leading to frustrated and disappointed visitors. Integration with 511, variable message signs on major roadways, improvements to the existing phone and web systems and better internal procedures to more smoothly and consistently activate these alert systems are recommended next steps.

15. SUBJECT TERMS
national park, park, traveler information systems, congestion, entrance stations

16. SECURITY CLASSIFICATION OF:			17. LIMITATION OF ABSTRACT	18. NUMBER OF PAGES	19a. NAME OF RESPONSIBLE PERSON Peter Steele, NER & Steve Herzog, SHEN
a. REPORT None	b. ABSTRACT None	c. THIS PAGE None	N/A	35	19b. TELEPHONE NUMBER *(Include area code)* 617-223-5130, NER / 540-999-3500 x3452, SHEN

Standard Form 298 (Rev. 8/98)
Prescribed by ANSI Std. Z39.18

As the nation's principal conservation agency, the Department of the Interior has the responsibility for most of our nationally owned public lands and natural resources. This includes fostering sound use of our land and water resources; protecting our fish, wildlife, and biological diversity; preserving the environmental and cultural values of our parks and historic places; and providing for the enjoyment of life through outdoor recreation. The department assesses our energy and mineral resources and works to ensure that their development is in the best interests of all our people by encouraging stewardship and citizen participation in their care. The department also has a major responsibility for American Indian reservation communities and for people who live in island territories under U.S. administration.

NPS 134/110081 August 2011

www.ingramcontent.com/pod-product-compliance
Lightning Source LLC
Chambersburg PA
CBHW081803170526
45167CB00008B/3313